The Longbow: The History of the Weapon that Revolutionized Warfare in the Middle Ages

By Charles River Editors

A medieval depiction of the Battle of Agincourt

About Charles River Editors

Charles River Editors provides superior editing and original writing services across the digital publishing industry, with the expertise to create digital content for publishers across a vast range of subject matter. In addition to providing original digital content for third party publishers, we also republish civilization's greatest literary works, bringing them to new generations of readers via ebooks.

Sign up here to receive updates about free books as we publish them, and visit Our Kindle Author Page to browse today's free promotions and our most recently published Kindle titles.

Introduction

A replica of an English longbow

In the time period between the fall of Rome and the spread of the Renaissance across the European continent, many of today's European nations were formed, the Catholic Church rose to great prominence, some of history's most famous wars occurred, and a social class system was instituted that lasted over 1,000 years. A lot of activity took place during a period frequently labeled derogatively as the "Dark Ages," and while that period of time is mostly referred to as the "Middle Ages" instead of the Dark Ages today, it has still retained the stigma of being a sort of lost period of time in which Western civilization made no worthwhile progress after the advances of the ancient civilizations of Greece and Rome.

In reality, this oversimplification of the Middle Ages overlooks the progress made in the studies of sciences and philosophy, especially during the High Middle Ages. It also ignores the fact that one of the most important inventions of the last millennium was created in Germany during the Late Middle Ages, the printing press, which allowed the Renaissance to move across the continent and help position Western Europe as the wealthiest region in the world.

If anything, the one aspect of the Middle Ages that has been romanticized is medieval warfare. Indeed, the Middle Ages have long sparked people's imaginations thanks to imagery of armored knights battling on horseback and armies of men trying to breach the walls of formidable castles. What is generally forgotten is that medieval warfare was constantly adapting to the times as leaders adopted new techniques and technology, and common infantry became increasingly important throughout the period. Starting around 1000 CE, there was a gradual consolidation of power in the region after the fragmentation of the Early Middle Ages, and it brought about the rise of more centralized states that could field large armies. The Normans, one of the first groups to do this, were notable for their discipline and organization, and it's little surprise that they were the last foreigners to successfully invade Britain under William the Conqueror in the mid-11th century.

Meanwhile, political and technological progress led to continuous change of tactics and equipment. Cavalry became ascendant, but at the Hundred Years' War's most famous battle, the Battle of Agincourt, archers formed a special part of the English army, beneath the men-at-arms but above the ordinary infantry. They wore leather body armor, sometimes with metal plates, and helmets or chainmail hoods. For close combat, they carried swords, mallets and daggers, including the misericord, a special type of dagger designed to slip between the armor plates of a fallen enemy and finish him off. The glory days of the heavily armored mounted knight had long since passed, and at Agincourt, English longbowmen and men-at-arms would decimate the flower of French chivalry, rendering the medieval cavalry charge little more than a romantic folly.

While the bow was used throughout ancient times and the Middle Ages, on mainland Europe it was mostly replaced by the crossbow in the early 13th century, but that would change with the introduction of the longbow, a more powerful weapon than the traditional hunting bows. The original longbowmen were Welshmen recruited by King Edward I of England after he conquered Wales, and the weapon got its name from the fact that it was almost as tall as the man using it. This gave it a longer draw and therefore more force, as longbows were generally made of yew, a strong and pliable wood. The longbow was cheap and easy to make, but they required extensive training to be used well, so in England, commoners were encouraged and at times required to practice archery. A statute of Richard II dating from 1388 reads, "Servants and Laborers shall have Bows and Arrows, and use the same the Sundays and Holydays, and leave all playing at tennis or foot-ball, and other games called coits, dice, casting of the stone, kaikles [skittles], and other such importune games."

The longbow's greatest day was at Agincourt in 1415, but the fact that this did not end the age of heavy plate cavalry indicated the longbow did have some limitations. For example, modern tests show that longbow arrows had trouble piercing plate armor, likely the main reason they were used as a massed weapon. With arrows raining down, it increased the chances of hitting a joint in the armor or an imperfection. Also, horse armor couldn't protect the entire animal and the knights would soon find themselves dismounted. At some battles like Agincourt, the knights foundered in soft earth, and as their horses fell and the men became confused and hampered by the arrows clanking off their armor, they got mired in the mud and the English infantry could move in and finish them off.

The Longbow: The History of the Weapon that Revolutionized Warfare in the Middle Ages

Ancient Bows

Although they are typically associated with medieval England, the longbow can trace its design back to at least 10000 BCE.[1] Exact estimates of when bows, as properly defined, were first crafted and used are difficult to make, but cave paintings depicting the use of bows may date to as early as the late Palaeolithic (c. 12000 BCE),[2] and arrowheads discovered around the Mediterranean may date as far back as 50000 BCE.[3]

The earliest extant bow was unearthed in the Alps in 1991 alongside the mummified remains of its owner, nicknamed "Otzi." Along with a dagger and a number of other primitive sharpening devices, numerous arrowheads were discovered in a leather quiver near Otzi's body.[4] The bow itself was made of just the heartwood of a tree, the kind of wood nearest to the center of a trunk that is the toughest and most durable to bending.[5] Fittingly, this material would continue to be favored even by more sophisticated bowyers for many years to come. Otzi's primitive bow appeared to have been incomplete at the time of his death (or murder, depending on the expert), but either way, the date of Otzi's death has been calculated to around the end of the 4th millennium BCE, making him the earliest definite user of a bow and arrow.

Otzi's possession is far from the only ancient example of a bow that historians have uncovered. Other early examples of usage include a skeleton of a young adult woman that was uncovered in northern Sudan dating to between 12000 and 4500 BCE. Although this dating is extremely wide, it is likely that the woman could be dated to the early times of the ancient kingdoms of Nubia. The woman's body was riddled with 21 chipped stone artifacts that were almost certainly arrowheads.[6]

Elsewhere, John France, Dean of the Faculty of Arts and Humanities at the University of Wales, noted in the *Journal of Medieval Military History* the Tomb of Inty, dating to roughly a millennium after Otzi's death. Inscribed in the tomb are depictions of early Egyptian warriors of the Old Kingdom opening fire upon Canaanite invaders using longbows. This depiction is notable for its apparent incorporation of longbows into proper battle strategy. The Egyptians are depicted shooting their arrows before dropping their bows to engage in melee combat with copper axes. France also noted that, despite the storm of arrows, the Canaanites continue to fight the Egyptians in close quarters. France suggests that this reveals some of the limitations in early bow-crafting. Perhaps the Egyptian bows were not as sophisticated as later designs used in the

---

[1] Loades, *War Bows*, 12.

[2] David Whetham, 'The English Longbow: A Revolution in Technology?' in Andrew Villalon and Donald Kagay (eds.), *The Hundred Years War (Part II)*, History of Warfare Volume 51, (Leiden/Boston: Brill, 2008), 213, n.5.

[3] Robert Hardy, *Longbow: A Social and Military History*, (London: Sutton Publishing, 1995), 12.

[4] Ursula Wierer, Simona Arrighi, Stefano Bertola, Günther Kaufmann, Benno Baumgarten, Annaluisa Pedrotti, Patrizia Pernter, Jacques Pelegrin, 'The Iceman's Lithic Toolkit: Raw Material, Technology, and Typology and Use,' PLOS ONE Vol. 13, Issue 6, (2018): 38.

[5] Loades, *War Bows*, 12.

[6] Whetham, 'The English Longbow,' 216.

ancient Near East, thus leading to their arrows having little penetrating effect. Either way, the Inty depiction offered a remarkable amount of information regarding ancient Egyptian bowmanship.[7]

A relief inside Ramesses II's Abu Simbel temple that depicts him firing arrows from a chariot during the Battle of Kadesh

---

[7] John France, 'The English Longbow, War, and Administration,' Journal of Medieval Military History Vol. 15, (2017): 216.

A depiction of Ramesses II firing arrows at the Nubians from his chariot

Mark Denny made an interesting observation regarding a recovered Assyrian bow dating to around 600 BCE. Denny's cross-section of the bow's wood reveals that even these ancient bows were carefully designed - the Assyrian bow was made out of two types of wood, three types of horn, a canvas of bone sinew and an outer protective layer of birch bark. The horn, which is more elastic than the wood, is placed on the belly of the bow, to allow for greater compression. The same design would be emulated by the English nearly 2,000 years later.[8] Denny pointed out that "we cannot escape the conclusion that a great deal of trial and error research and development went into these machines, which tells us something about how important they were."[9]

Independently of the Assyrians, Native Americans developed similar designs for their bows. Ancient Inuit people crafted bows strung with sinew at the back of the bow, and the sinew is applied to the bow when wet. As it dries, it shrinks, allowing for increased resistance to tension.

Perhaps the most effective bows to employ this design are the recurve bows of the Persians and Turks. These were the first bows to have the body of the bow curve *away* from the archer, allowing for more tension and an increase in draw weight. Such bows, known as Turkish flight bows, are recorded to have allegedly have a range of over 2,500 feet (the modern record for a flight bow is currently 1,145 meters).[10]

---

[8] Denny, *Ingenium*, 7.

[9] Ibid.

[10] Denny notes that bow making was a "lost art" up until 1910 and early reconstructions of Turkish flight bows only amounted to half the alleged distance (*Ingenium*, 8). Modern reconstructions use far more effective materials such as nylon, fiberglass, or spring steel. These materials, though affective today, make it difficult to estimate how far an ancient bow could have actually shot. Still, there is no reason that the ancient Turks and Persians could not have reached up to 800 meters using their designs.

It is somewhat remarkable that historians have found ancient bows in modern times given that they are made of wood and wood decomposes. Most forms of preservations that ensure the survival of such tools come from bogs, silts, and other oxygen-free environments. Such an environment in Denmark yielded 40 longbows dating to the 4th century CE, and these were believed to have been military-grade longbows due to a spear-like tip attached to each end of the bow. This design would have allowed the owners to transition from ranged to close quarters fighting quickly, with the bow acting as a spear instead. This suggests that the owners were anticipating engaging in hand-to-hand combat.[11]

Prior to these discoveries, historians in the first half of the 20th century believed that Wales was the land of the longbow's origin.[12] This mostly stems from the work of British military historian Charles Oman, who argued for the longbow's absorption into English militaries in his 1924 work *The Art of War in the Middle Ages*. Subsequent historians, such as John Morris, Matthew Strickland, Robert Hardy, and J. C. Holt, went on to find much earlier depictions of longbows, many of which have already been cited above.[13]

While the position that Wales is the origin of the longbow is certainly no longer the case, archers operating in Wales did have a substantial role to play in the evolution and perfection of the warbow amongst the larger numbers of the English military, as will be discussed below. As Whetham put it, "Edward I did not introduce a new weapon to the English army following his subjugation of the Welsh. Instead, the English developed an appreciation for what this *old* weapon could do when employed in significant numbers."[14] It is clear from the above cases that the longbow was not necessarily a new invention in medieval weaponry and technology, as the means, motive, and material to create "primitive" longbows were present for thousands of years prior to the wars fought by the English.

This also plays into more scholarly discussions concerning the origin of the longbow, such as the idea that there was a deterministic evolution of the bow from a shorthand weapon (probably akin to a composite bow) into the larger, more effective longbow designed for massive range. Scholars such as Matthew Prestwich, John France, Kelly DeVries and the aforementioned Strickland affirm that longbows were standard bows throughout the Middle Ages, rather than being a development of the 13th and 14th centuries and replacing an earlier "shortbow." Some adherents of the revisionist view, in particular Strickland, assert that the shortbow itself never existed, saying that the longbow, in some form, was always part of the English ranged military, even prior to the defeat of the Welsh at the hands of Edward I. This stands in contrast to the traditional view that the English longbow was a product of the "14th century infantry revolution."[15]

---

[11] Loades, *War Bows*, 12; Loades, *The Longbow*, 7.

[12] Anthony Bruce, *A Bibliography of British Military History: From the Roman Invasions to the Restoration, 1660,* (London/Paris/New York: Saur, 1981), 310; Whetham, 'The English Longbow,' 215.

[13] See France, 'The English Longbow,' 218-220.

[14] Whetham, 'The English Longbow,' 232; emphasis his

[15] Cliff Rogers, The Development of the Longbow in Late Medieval England and 'Technological Determinism,'

That said, this revisionist stance has not gone without question. For example, Cliff Rogers, professor of history at the United States Military Academy, contends that the "revisionist stance is incorrect, and that the longbow, which first saw widespread use only in the 14th century, was indeed a different and significantly more effective weapon than the shorter bows common before then."[16] Rogers has specifically critiqued Prestwich in his review of Strickland's thesis in *The Great Warbow* (2005), which was co-authored by classical actor Robert Hardy, known for his roles in *Harry Potter* and *All Creatures Great and Small*. Strickland and Hardy affirmed that the longbow was not a "new" weapon developed in medieval Europe during Edward I's reign, a thesis that Prestwich thoroughly agreed to. Rogers states that "Prestwich's willingness to accept Strickland and Hardy's case so completely is surprising given his own observation in the same review that 'it is curious that casualty levels appear to have increased as defensive armour became more sophisticated in the later middle ages, particularly if, as is argued here, there was little development in bow technology.'"[17] Rogers supports the traditionalist position by appealing to tapestries depicting archers in battle from prior to the Hundred Year's War, noting that "unambiguous depictions of near-longbows or longbows between the 10th century and the 14th century are exceedingly rare."[18] Rogers concludes "the iconographic evidence provides confirmation for the traditional belief that for two centuries or more following the Norman Conquest the bows used in England, like those used elsewhere, were normally short or medium bows, not longbows."[19]

The current state of the debate remains at an impasse, but most historians lean in favor of the revisionist position.[20] Only the development of future scholarship will help bring clarity and conclusion to the question of how the longbow developed in English history.

The Longbow's Design

Early forms of the longbow before its "perfection" by the Welsh and English militaries were made with composite materials such as horn and sinew,[21] but the primary material was, of course, wood, which was never in short supply in Europe. The intention for the bow-slinger was to use a material that would be able to sufficiently conduct the kinetic energy generated by releasing the string.

Journal of Medieval History, Vol. 37, Issue 3 (2011): 321.

[16] Ibid, 323.

[17] Ibid, 322, n.12.

[18] Ibid, 338.

[19] Ibid, 339.

[20] Strickland's book has turned the tide of the scholarship, but many traditionalists remain unconvinced. Some have criticised Hardy's contributions, with Tobias Capwell saying that they "suffer somewhat from an overly sentimental perspective" (Review of *From Hastings to the Mary Rose: The Great Warbow*, Matthew Strickland and Robert Hardy, Journal of Conflict Archaeology Volume 2, Number 1 (2013): 212). Other reviewers found it an illuminating and interesting study of an important aspect of mediaeval history" (Anonymous, Review of *From Hastings to the Mary Rose: The Great Warbow*. Matthew Strickland and Robert Hardy, Contemporary Review, Volume 287 (2005), 123).

[21] Whetham, 'The English Longbow,' 214.

During the Middle Ages, the most efficient source for bow timber was the yew tree, and yew proved to be especially popular in England from the late 15th century. Yorkist and Lancaster kings requested the material from Southern Italy, where the best yew was believed to have been produced.[22] Yew heartwood provided the best resistance to compression and yew sapwood also provides the best tension relief, and so was placed on the back of the bow to prevent it snapping during drawback.[23] Alternatives to Italian yew included wych elm and yew produced in Poland, but those resources were not as strong as the yew produced in Italy. The Polish yew, in particular, was grown in colder conditions and was therefore less capable of handling the stresses of usage. However, that inferiority also meant it was less expensive than the high-quality yew produced in Italy, leading to a large demand for Polish yew.[24]

When it came to crafting the arrows, many materials were available and a variety were used in in communities across Europe. Robert Ascham, a personal tutor for Edward VI and Elizabeth I, composed the first English book of archery and bowyer, the *Toxophilus* (1545). It is a classic work that continues to be used and cited in crafting to this very day.[25] Ascham wrote that ash wood was the most appropriate wood choice for the shaft of an arrow, noting that it was "swiftest and again heavy to give a great stroke, which asp[en] will not do."[26] Nevertheless, aspen wood was commonly used to produce arrows, much to Ascham's chagrin. Aspen was inferior to ash (at least in Ascham's eyes) because it was lighter, and the weight of the projectile had direct influence on the force of the shot. Nevertheless, aspen was very common in the late Tudor period. In fact, roughly 77% of the arrows retrieved from the *Mary Rose*, an English warship that was sunk in 1545 during the Battle of the Solent, were crafted from aspen, with another nine different types of wood making up the last 23%.[27]

The string of a bow was also an essential component to get correct. Most strings in medieval bows were made with hemp or flax.[28] As mentioned above during the Battle of Crecy, archers had to ensure the strings remained dry as to avoid making them slack. Crossbows, for all of their shortcomings, had leather strings and were much more effective in the rain.

The rear of the arrow is known as the fletching, where feathers taken from a bird are attached for the sake of increasing the arrow's aerodynamism. The feathers are aligned in a circular motion down the body of the arrow, which causes it to spin once loosed from a bow. Although this may seem counterproductive to laypeople, it allows the arrow to capture more air as it flies, increasing the range of the shot. However, an archer does not want to have too much spin on the arrow, or it will spin away from the desired target. Thus, creating the fletching is a very delicate

---

[22] Loades, *War Bows*, 20.
[23] Whetham, 'The English Longbow,' 214.
[24] Loades, *War Bows*, 20.
[25] See, for example, Ian Pope, *Modern Longbow Design & Toxophilus: Longbow Design Refined By Ascham, A Voice From the Past* (2011).
[26] Loades, *War Bows*, 26.
[27] Ibid.
[28] 'The Welsh and English Longbow,' 6.

procedure and perhaps the most vital to creating an arrow. A faulty fletching can ruin the perfect shot; therefore, a number of factors must be taken into account by the bowyer when creating the bow's projectile. For example, the larger the feathers in the fletching, larger feathers straighten the arrow, allowing for a greater control of the extent of the spinning and thus increases accuracy.

On the other hand, smaller feathers produce less air resistance and can allow an arrow to travel faster.[29] The bowyer should also ensure that the feathers used in making the fletching (typically just three) are from the location of the same bird and all of the same size. Even slight variations can have an enormous impact on the efficiency and accuracy of the arrow. Whetham records a study which was conducted by Royal Military College of Science, where one set of arrows had their fletching altered with tiny pieces of foil glued to the feathers. The overall differences observed resulted in an average accuracy error of two metres using the altered arrows.[30] It would thus be important for the bowyers to painstakingly craft the fletching and ensure that only the most perfect of arrows would be sent off to the battlefield.

Arrows are loosed at an acceleration of 300g, and within a few milliseconds of being loosed, most of the energy stored in the string is transferred to the arrow itself.[31] As a result, ensuring that the right material is used in constructing the piercing tip of an arrow was essential.

The simplest and most common design for an arrowhead is the square bodkin. Used extensively during the Middle Ages, it is a simple steel tip protruding from the wood of the arrow. The iconic square section and the small cross section made it the standard arrow to use in most activities, whether recreational or military.[32]

Alternatively, broadhead arrows were used specially in combat. Larger and more deadly than bodkin arrows, broadheads had three or four sharp blades protruding from the arrowhead. This was to maximize damage in a target by causing extra bleeding. It was also more gruesomely designed to prevent the target from removing the arrowhead, as the backward-pointing blades would tear the flesh of the victim should they try to remove it, causing further injury.

Apart from the normal iron-tipped arrows, incendiary arrows were also favored strategically at times by archers in the Middle Ages, and there were three types of incendiary arrows during this period. The first was the cage arrow, for which a simple cage stuffed full of wool or hemp saturated with a flammable compound would be carried around by the archer. At the onset of a battle, the archer could quickly place the cage and use it to ignite regular arrows and fire them. Although incapable of dealing much extra damage, the cage type had the benefit of being a quick option for an archer. Thus, situations such as ambushes could be readily dealt with by archers

---

[29] Whetham, 'The English Longbow,' 225.
[30] Ibid.
[31] Denny, *Ingenium*, 2.
[32] 'The Welsh and English Longbow,' 6.

using the cage -type.

The second incendiary arrow was the bag-type, which was much more reliable than the cage-type but required much more preparation. An extra-long bodkin arrow would pierce a canvas sausage of flammable paste. These would need to be made in advance so that the archer could ignite the paste and use readily in combat. The third type is essentially a further modification of the second: the bag-type coated with resin. Further adding to the flammability and reliability of the bag-type arrow, the resin would seal the flammable canvas, preventing it from getting wet. The resin also ensured that the flames would not be put out by the speed of the arrow's loosing. By the time the arrow landed, the resin would likely have been burned up, thus igniting the flammable canvas underneath, dealing the real damage to the target. This, of course, would require even more time to prepare and could leave the archer vulnerable during preparation.[33]

Crafting a bow is a delicate process, and it was outlined Loades in his monograph *War Bows*.[34] Firstly, small staves of felled timber would be split into square shaped blanks. The split timber is next shaved on a shooting plane and then rounded by a finishing plane to create the arrow's cylindrical shape. It may also have been used to ensure that each arrow was of the same diameter. Following the creation of the arrow body, the shaft is smoothed using abrasives such as sandstone. At the rear of the arrow, a nock is sawn through the center of the shaft, allowing its user to link the arrow to the string. Following the nock, feathers from either a goose, swan, or peacock are collected for the fletching at the rear of the arrow. These must be carefully selected, as mites that are often found of birds could infest and destroy whole crates full of feathers that are intended to be used in arrow crafting. The feathers are cut up to the appropriate size and shape to allow for best aerodynamic ability and then attached to the rear of the arrow. This is done either by using glue made from rabbit hide or bound together by silk or linen. Sometimes, both were utilized to ensure that the fletching was durable enough for shooting. To prevent the aforementioned mite infestation, early insect repellents crafted from beeswax and copper sulphate were coated onto the feathers after they formed the fletching. Then, finally, the head of the arrow is sharpened forward to create a wooden arrowhead before the real arrowhead is attached. The final product would be on average around 6'6" long, and the arrows would be up to a full meter long.[35]

Given the exertions required, an individual wielding a bow and arrow in battle had to be at the peak of human physicality and mentality. Dexterity was required to sling and reload with speed and efficiency, patience and judgement were needed to search for a target and know when the opportune time was to loose an arrow, and stamina was essential when the front lines failed and the archers became the target of better equipped infantrymen looking for easy kills. As Loades noted, "To be able to nock, draw to full length and, crucially, shoot rapidly under the extreme

---

[33] Loades, *War Bows*, 29.
[34] Ibid, 24-25.
[35] 'The Welsh and English Longbow,' 6.

condition of combat – facing an enemy charge – required not only a special kind of calm courage, but also a muscle memory drilled to an unfaltering precision and reliability, something that only came with practice."[36]

Once again, the sunken *Mary Rose* gave researchers insights into the physiques of the Tudor archers. Before its discovery, most historians assumed that the upper draw weight of a typical longbow would be a pull of around 100 pounds,[37] but the bows found on the *Mary Rose* made historians realize that 100 pounds would be the minimum draw weight, being supplanted by a maximum of 180 pounds. This therefore makes roughly 150 pounds the average draw weight of Tudor archers.[38] Additionally, the draw weights would have been too much even for the most physically able archers. The bodies of two archers recovered from the Mary Rose exhibited signs of deformities, both on their left arms and spines, typical signs of prolonged careers as archers. This is even more remarkable since both archers were only in their 20s.[39] Archers, therefore, must have been significantly stronger to wield these older types of bows than what had been previously expected by historians. Whetham explained, "It is highly doubtful that the majority of modern enthusiasts would be willing or even able to put themselves through the type of training regime that could inflict the physical deformities similar to those discovered on the *Mary Rose* archers."[40]

Given the danger, the English governments had to motivate the average Englishman to put in the work and effort to become an archer in service of the king. One of these was the decent pay that they received, as well as the prospect of looting precious rewards on the battlefield after a skirmish. Perhaps the best incentive was the gradual development of an archery culture amongst the English lower classes, because, as France noted, "the bow was used by a very wide range of people for a number of purposes."[41] Men who became proficient in the art of archery would have gained significant social status, thus leading them to become renowned soldiers on the battlefield and as heroes of war.[42] It should be noted, therefore, that archers were, at the very least, yeomen - free men who came from the lower classes, largely from farming communities. The Assize of Arms of 1252 required all "citizens, burgesses, free tenants, villeins and others from 15 to 60 years of age" to be armed.[43] Serfs and slaves could not and did not serve as archers in the English military.[44]

---

[36] Loades, *War Bows*, 33.
[37] As assumed by 'The Welsh and English Longbow,' 7.
[38] Whetham, 'The English Longbow,' 222.
[39] Ibid, 223.
[40] Ibid.
[41] France, 'The English Longbow,' 221.
[42] Loades, 36.
[43] France, 'The English Longbow,' 221.
[44] 'The Welsh and English Longbow,' 6.

Defenses

In Loades' essential study of the longbow, he noted that any assessment of the longbow's lethal potential must encompass an understanding of how armour developed to deal with the threat.[45] Indeed, a great amount of historical and scientific literature has been produced both theoretically and practically to determine how ancient armorers honed their craft to counter the increasing threat of longbowmen and their arrows.

The iconic image of a medieval knight would naturally give the impression that such a soldier, clad from head to toe in a coat of thick steel, would be immune to any projectiles launched in his direction. After all, the armor provided immense protection for the wearer in close-quarters combat, and as the development of technology continued, sheets of iron were improving as to their thickness. Only small amounts of residual carbon in the iron made it difficult to harden and temper it into the shape desired by the maker. By the 15th century, iron was more available in copious amounts, leading to the forging of alloys of iron and steel with significant amounts of carbon. These alloys could be heat-treated in various ways that allowed it to be hardened, all without increasing the weight. It would be further reinforced with a thick layer of leather undercoats that had been shaped to the wearer's specifications (known as cuir-bouilli[46]). This would provide an increased depth to the armor that would reduce injury should the armor be penetrated. By the 14th century, such kinds of leather reinforcement were mass produced, heralding a fundamental shift in armor design. This would undoubtedly be effective against both infantrymen and archers.

Recent studies have shown, however, that even a knight in shining armor may have been helpless against the volley of arrows from a medieval longbow. Research by Mark Stretton of the English War Bow Society conducted a number of tests on replicated knight armour by launching arrows from a typical medieval bow to see the penetration rate and how deep the wounds would have been. Stretton's results were shocking, as "arrows shot from powerful longbows punch through virtually everything put in front of them, and they do so to depths that would deliver mortal wounds."[47] It seems that no warrior on the battlefield was safe from the feared archers, not even the noblest knights. Given the lack of protection that the knights' armor provided against these arrows, Whetham described the longbow as a "medieval machine gun."[48]

That said, Stretton's evaluation has been criticized for not accurately replicating the conditions in which such an incident would occur. It is one thing to fire an arrow against a still-standing mannequin wearing the armour, it is another to hit a moving target in the middle of an active battlefield. What if the battle was taking place in the rain? What if the archer was ill or wounded in some way? What about the experience of the archer? What if the target had a shield,

[45] Loades, *The Longbow*, 6.
[46] Ibid, 10.
[47] As cited by Loades, *War Bows*, 13.
[48] Whetham, 'The English Longbow,' 213.

something which posed a significant barrier to the archer from hitting his target.[49] Such factors cannot be replicated today with any degree of confidence. As France puts it, range, weather, the quality of the bow, and the nature of the arrow are obvious variables. Above all, of course, are the quality and abilities of the archer himself. It is for this reason that before the development of really effective firearms, battle was decided at close quarters by troops, cavalry or infantry, fighting in close quarter with edged weapons."[50] Loades adds that "the isolated conditions of the testing ground never fully replicate the complex and chaotic circumstances of a battlefield."[51]

Additionally, Stretton's tests found that there was one type of garment that could afford ample resistance to the arrows of the bow: chainmail. This light garb of interlocking metal chains proved invaluable for light infantry and archers in resisting the blades of their enemies. Combined with the outer shell of a suit of armor, the warrior would be nearly invulnerable, albeit weighed down.

The chainmail's effectiveness against arrows, however, should not be overstated. If an arrow was launched at a perfect 90-degree angle, the chainmail would prove to be of little resistance. Chainmail is most effective against arrows shot at inopportune angles, and, if the arrow was to penetrate, the mail would absorb a great deal of the delivering energy.[52] The mail would also not be alone - most soldiers wearing chainmail would have underneath it a "coat of plates" or "jack of plates," a leather or linen base with a thin metal plate riveted inside it. The jack of plates was fitted with multiple small plates that not only overlapped from improved resistance, but also allowed for improved flexibility. Such types of armour became increasingly popular among archers in the 15th century, as it allowed them to be sufficiently protected whilst retaining the necessary flexibility needed for loosing arrows.[53]

Although chainmail may have assisted in protecting the man under the armour, it would do him no good if the armour proved to be a cumbersome source of great weight to him. Cliff Rogers notes that it would take such a heavily armoured man roughly two minutes to travel 200 metres. In that time, a single archer could loose a significant number of arrows at his position (between 8 and 15 if Roger's numbers are correct). Additionally, the archer would most likely not be alone. If there were, for example, 5,000 archers (the likely number of which who were present at the Battle of Agincourt and were largely responsible for the English victory there[54]), then this would result in up to 1,000 arrows being loosed every second at the approaching host. Casualties would be inevitable, not to mention the psychological stress of seeing allied soldiers fall quickly around oneself. It would naturally lead to a collapse of unit cohesion, rendering any armour useless if it

---

[49] Loades considers the shield "the most significant item of defence equipment against arrows" (*War Bows*, 13).
[50] France, 'The English Longbow,' 216.
[51] Loades, *The Longbow*, 8.
[52] Loades, *War Bows*, 13.
[53] Loades, *The Longbow*, 10-11.
[54] The Hampton Roads Military History regards it as the "decisive factor" contributing to the English victory over the more numerous French ('The Welsh and English Longbow' in Hampton Roads Military History Vol. 1 (2007)): 6.

had not already been penetrated by an arrow.[55]

Are Shields Enough?

Another question remains: what good would a shield do against arrows? We have already seen that the most essential defence against arrows – a knight's armour – is not necessarily impervious to the bow's ranged projectiles. Perhaps modern depictions of shields against arrows (such as in the HBO series Game of Thrones where the character Jon Snow uses a single shield to block three arrows) have also been grossly overstated.

Loades considers the shield to be "the most significant item of defensive equipment against arrows."[56] Unlike the yew or ash used respectively for the bow and arrow, shields were often fashioned from solid blocks of lime wood (known as basswood in North America). This kind of timber was light in weight, making it the perfect choice for a shield. Sycamore was also felled for the production of shields, despite it being much heavier.[57] The weight was a price that a shield crafter was willing to pay, as the harder wood of a sycamore would provide a great advantage to defending against arrows.

Whether they were made with sycamore or lime wood, the finished product would be reinforced with other materials to increase its energy absorption. The underside and rims of a shield would be laminated with parchment, rawhide, leather, or hairpelt. These would make holding the shield more comfortable and would reduce the shock of an arrow impact. On the front of a shield would be a mosaic made of horn or bone, many of which still survive in extant examples. Combining all the features of a shield together, they add several extra layers of depth to a shield which would help challenge arrow penetration.[58]

It would seem that the shield's effectiveness against arrows was not to be understated. A properly fashioned shield could provide exemplary defence against a barrage of arrows. As noted by the English chronicler, Geoffrey le Baker, French soldiers at the Battle of Poitiers in 1356 advanced in a close formation, "protecting their bodies with joined shields, [and] turned their faces away from missiles. So the archers emptied their quivers in vain."[59]

The Middle Ages

The Middle Ages span a vast amount of time, from the era of Rome's collapse to the beginning of the Tudor period in England. In the earliest period of this era, there were early mentions of the longbow being used by Celtic tribes, which provide an important but confusing insight into the

---

[55] Cliff Rogers, 'The Efficacy of the English Longbow: A Reply to Kelly DeVries,' War in History Volume 5, No. 2 (April 1998): 235; see also Whetham, 'The English Longbow,' 231.
[56] Loades, *The Longbow*, 9.
[57] Ibid.
[58] Ibid.
[59] Ibid.

longbow's European development because the words that the Celts used to describe the longbow could also refer to some form of throwing spear. As a result, some scholars believe that the Norman invaders of 1066 introduced the first proper longbows to the British Isles, while others argue there is sufficient evidence, despite its sparsity, to demonstrate that the longbow had been used prior to William the Conqueror's invasion. The former option has become unfavourable in recent decades, both due to the prehistoric evidence of the longbow in England and Wales, and also because of the few Anglo-Saxon texts that are much clearer in their descriptions of longbows. For example, Offrid (or Osfrith), the son of the Northumbrian King Edwin (586 – c. 633), was killed by an arrow in a battle against the Welsh Mercians.[60]

The use of the longbow amongst Vikings as a hunting weapon has been established, although it is unclear if it was used as a weapon in combat. Referred to amongst the Vikings as a "strongbow," Scandinavian longbow remains have been discovered among remains of Viking vessels that crossed the North Sea, such as the Nydam ship. These designs, as expected, were all taller than the men that would have carried them. By the 8th century,

Vikings had begun to spread from Scandinavia to the British Isles, and they almost certainly used the warbow. Surviving law edicts from the English villages that had been raided by the Vikings place limits on the amount of longbow that can be issued to the peasants for defense against Viking invaders. It would be very unusual if the Vikings themselves had not also used the longbow in attacks if the villagers used it for defense.[61]

Some periods of English history around this time were dominated by Danish rule. Some of note, 876-954 (when Danish kings ruled York and the north of Britain), as well as 1013 and 1045 (the rule of the Danish House Canute over England) must have encouraged a large amount of cultural sharing between Danes and Angles, whether it was willful or not. This probably led to the proliferation of the longbow from Wessex to Jutland and to Halogaland.[62]

The Welsh, in particular, found it very useful in guerrilla warfare against the English,[63] and Whetham believed that the Welsh had mastered the warbow in their efforts against the English before it was utilized by the English themselves.[64] In 1056, just 10 years before the Battle of Hastings, the *Abingdon Chronicle* detailed a Welsh ambush against the English and claimed the Welsh archers were so accurate that "the English people fled before even a spear had been thrown."[65]

At Hastings itself, archers were used sporadically by William the Conqueror's Normans, and

---

[60] Whetham, 'The English Longbow,' 217-18.
[61] Ibid, 218.
[62] Ibid.
[63] Loades, *War Bows*, 10-11.
[64] Whetham, 'The English Longbow,' 213.
[65] Ibid, 219.

the battle demonstrated to the conquering invaders that the archers were not as important as the infantry. William pulled his archers back to allow his swordsmen to engage in melee, and when Harold Godwinson did the opposite, placing his archers forward to open fire on the Norman infantry, they were run down by the Norman cavalry.[66]

The longbow's popularity was felt strongly across class divisions. The early tales of Robin Hood were cemented in this period as the longbow found popularity. It is also why the longbow found little initial support in France in the same period. The idea that the a commoner could slay a veteran knight with a few simple sticks and some string was abhorrent to the more rigid ruling French classes. To certain breeds of Englishmen, however, "the idea that strength and skill can triumph over wealth and status is a powerful one."[67]

Additionally, many poor bowyers were conscripted by the English army to produce the bows, which led the longbow to become a symbol of class empowerment in medieval England.[68] Many impoverished individuals found that their one and only useful trade was that of bowmanship, thus leading to a constant supply of archers for many European militaries. Combined with the offer of hope that these lower-class individuals could metaphorically cast off the yoke of their rich lords, this no doubt contributed to England's large numbers of skilled archers.

European bowmen would be utilized far from their native homes. During the Third Crusade, at the Battle of Arsuf, Richard the Lionheart strategically used his archers and infantry to surround his cavalry and reduce the efficiency of Saladin's mounted archers. One of Saladin's generals commented, "The enemy army was already in formation with the infantry surrounding it like a wall, wearing solid iron corselets and full-length well-made chain-mail, so that arrows were falling on them with no effect [...] I saw various individuals amongst the Franks with ten arrows fixed in their backs, pressing on in this fashion quite unconcerned."[69]

It was around the late 13th century that the warbow began to come into its prime. This period saw the maximum use of the longbow in its history, being utilized across various cultures and geographical regions, especially in Europe. The longstanding myth that the longbow had to battle its way to the forefront of ranged weapons against the crossbow has a small number of supporters today, but most scholars assert there was a continual usage of the longbow from before the development of the crossbow. Ultimately, of course, crossbows fell into disuse due to the effectiveness of the longbow.[70]

No more explicitly is the longbow's touch on history found than at the Battle of Crecy in 1346. During his campaign in France in the early years of the Hundred Years' War, Edward III's army

---

[66] France, 'The English Longbow,' 216.
[67] Loades, *The Longbow*, 4.
[68] Loades, *War Bows*, 8.
[69] France, 'The English Longbow,' 216.
[70] See Rogers, 'Development,' 326-32.

found itself hounded by the much larger force of the French King Phillip VI. Roughly 10,000 Englishmen faced off against 20,000-30,000 Frenchmen. Edward had no cavalry to speak of, while Phillip had around 10,000 mounted knights.[71] It seemed to be an inevitable defeat for the English, who were on hostile soil, surrounded, and outnumbered.

The initial contact of the battle began with a standoff between the English longbowmen and the Italian Genoese crossbowmen, mercenaries hired by the French. Like much of the situation at Crecy, the battle initially seemed to be in favor of the French forces, and a sudden downpour of rain meant that the English archers had to de-string their bows to prevent the strings from slacking. The Italian crossbowmen, who had strings made from leather, had no such problem and began their attack upon the English.[72]

Despite the rainy conditions, which made it more difficult for the archers to sling their arrows, the Genoese were repelled. The crossbows had shorter range than the superior longbow, and the highly trained English archers had a higher rate of fire (more than three times greater).[73] This reload rate was reduced even further when the crossbowmen were forced to press their stirrups into the muddy ground.[74] The Genoese crossbowmen also lacked their defensive barricades (known as pavises), which were back with the French convoy along with their ammunition reserves.[75]

Eventually, the Genoese crossbowmen fled the first engagement, angering the nobles watching on horseback from a distance. The leader of the cavalry, Charles II of Alencon, began an impromptu horse charge, but the disorderly nature of the cavalry and the retreating crossbowmen led to many of the Genoese being trampled by the charging horsemen. Some of the mounted nobles even cut down the Italians for fleeing the battle.[76]

When the cavalry came upon the English archers, their unprotected horses fared poorly, and many horsemen were spilled from their horses and crushed underneath their mounts. Horses that were wounded fled the battle in panic, all while English archers continued their volleys of arrows, felling more and more French soldiers. The battle continued well into the night as the French attempted the same tactic multiple times, each time being thwarted by the English archers. Eventually, the stubborn French nobles abandoned the battle, resulting in a remarkable English victory. Mark Denny describes Crecy as a "stand-off victory, won at a distance by the archers."[77]

---

[71] Denny, *Ingenium*, 3.

[72] Kelly DeVries, "The Implications of the Anonimo Romano Account of the Battle of Crécy" in Gregory I. Halfond (ed.). *The Medieval Way of War: Studies in Medieval Military History in Honor of Bernard S. Bachrach.* (London: Routledge, 2015), 309–322.

[73] Michael Prestwich, "The Battle of Crécy" in Andrew Ayton, & Philip Preston, (eds.), *The Battle of Crécy, 1346,* (Woodbridge, Suffolk: Boydell Press, 2007), 139–157.

[74] DeVries, 'Implications,' 318-19.

[75] Henri de Wailly, *Crécy 1346: Anatomy of a Battle,* (Poole: Blandford Press, 1987), 66.

[76] Denny, *Ingenium*, 3.

The English victory was decisive from a tactical standpoint, but in the long run it proved strategically inconsequential. The Breton War lasted 24 years before ending with the Treaty of Guerande, which confirmed John de Montfort in the duchy. French resources had been depleted, and King Charles V of France reluctantly accepted the results as a *fait accompli*. The English now had a power base in Brittany, but the war between England and France was not over, and the French suffered a devastating defeat at Poitiers on September 19, 1356. Edward's son, Edward the Black Prince, captured John II, who had succeeded Charles in 1350.

John was taken to England until a colossal ransom was paid, and France descended into chaos. With the kingdom crippled by rebellion and by the ransom, the dauphin (crown prince) Charles negotiated with the English. The Treaty of Bretigny, ratified on October 24, 1360, gave Calais and Aquitaine to Edward in his own right in exchange for the renunciation of claims on the French throne.

Regardless of strategic importance, Crecy was seen as a watershed for class struggle. Hundreds of nobles on their horseback were slaughtered by the English peasant archers, and that kind of victory sent shockwaves around Europe, indicating to individuals of every conviction and background that they could make a stand against the ruling gentry and assert their independence. As Denny put it, "The days of chivalry died on the field at Crecy."[78]

Still, it was important for European armies not to overemphasize the usefulness of archers in all settings, and in some battles, archers proved to be of little use in determining the outcome of major battles. For example, at Benevento in 1266, Manfred of Sicily is recorded to have had a very large host of archers at his disposal, but the battle was ultimately decided by the knights. Another example was the Battle of the Golden Spurs in 1302. The French had roughly 1,000 crossbowmen against 900 on the Flemish side, but they played a negligible role and there were apparently no ordinary archers. Most notably, very shortly after, Edward mustered very large numbers of archers for his disastrous battle at Bannockburn against Robert I in 1314.[79] At the Battle of Flodden Field in 1513, an English army was confronted by an invading Scottish force led by heavily armoured pikemen, and though English archers disrupted the enemy's assault, they failed to halt the advance. As the English chronicler Edward Hall noted, "They abode the most dangerous shot of arrowes, which sore them noyed, and yet it hit them in some bare place it dyd them no hurt."[80]

Curiously, during the reign of Edward III, bows were banned from being used at night due to the risk of misfiring. In 1399, an individual named Tom Coton was appointed "Maker of the King's Bows" and was charged with ensuring the quality of the material being used to produce the warbows being supplied to the English arsenal at the Tower of London.[81] It may be that the

---

[77] Denny, *Ingenium*, 5.
[78] Ibid.
[79] See further examples in France, 'The English Longbow,' 217.
[80] Phillips, 'Longbow and Hackbutt,' 579.

sudden defeat of Edward III's predecessor at Bannockburn contributed to the refusal to allow archers operating at night and in major cities. It is unknown whether the ineptitude of the archers was blamed for the English defeat, but it is possible that this led to a decline in popularity amongst English military circles. Nevertheless, this remains only conjecture.[82]

France presented the inconsistent effectiveness of archers in an appropriate way: "[A]rchers were not invariably present in battle, and often were not very effective. Now, it has to be admitted that our sources for battles were usually aristocratic, and therefore focused on the knights and leaders. Even so, enough is known to make it clear that the effectiveness of archery fluctuated enormously. And yet, in the 14th and 15th centuries archers proved to be immensely effective against knights wearing highly effective and very sophisticated armour, much of which was specifically designed with oblique surfaces to deflect arrows."[83]

Historians are left to determine whether something drastic happened in between these few hundred years that caused archers to become more effective. France's summary of the scholarship on this issue embodies this confusion, observing, "This is clearly not merely an issue of technology, for I am sure that Strickland and Hardy are right, that powerful longbows were known before 1300."[84] It hardly seems likely, given the undeniably impressive battles like Crecy, that were won almost singlehandedly by ranged fighters. France's explanation may be the most convincing - the gradual improvement of the archer as a battle soldier may be attributed to the improvement of military strategy, training, administration, and high demand for more soldiers.

During the reign of Edward, demand for archers increased due to his imperial ambitions, which had previously not been needed in such demands in the country. The upper classes rallied behind Edward's ambitions, but the need for large infantry forces demanded conscription of the lower classes. This did not work due to the openness to abuse that the system had, so Edward turned his attention to recruiting fewer but more skilled archers. He simply did not have the time, means, or infrastructure to train new archers, but reliance upon the native skills of the lower classes meant that Edward would gain good numbers of effective archers without the need to train new archers. By the end of the 13th century, England had become rather wealthy, which gave the country the opportunity to use even more of these native archers and bows. The excess money could be spent on improving technologies, hence the evolution of the archer and the bow itself. In combination with an ever-evolving archery culture that was (and still is) especially prominent in England, it is not difficult to see how strong France's explanation is in demonstrating how archery developed and improved in the Middle Ages.

Agincourt remains one of the most famous battles in English history, and it represents the peak of the longbow's fame.

---

[81] Loades, *War Bows*, 19-20.
[82] Loades notes that bowyers too were forbidden to work after dark (Loades, *War Bows*, 27).
[83] France, 'The English Longbow,' 217.
[84] Ibid, 222.

On October 8, 1415, the remnants of Henry V's army, which had been campaigning in the north of France, headed north to devastate the coast and return to England from Calais. He left 1,200 men to garrison Harfleur under the command of his uncle, Thomas, Earl of Dorset, while the remainder that marched out consisted of just 1,000 men-at-arms and 5,000 longbowmen. They were split into three divisions under the king himself, Edmund the first Duke of York, and Richard de Vere, Earl of Oxford.

From the beginning, plenty of subordinates recognized the apparent foolhardiness of the venture. The small English army was tired, poorly-fed, and still suffering from the effects of disease. The heavy autumn rains were setting in and would considerably slow its progress. The troops had only provisions for eight days, and when that ran out there would be little food to be taken from the countryside. Nevertheless, they made for the village of Blanchetaque, about 100 miles northeast of Harfleur, where they determined to cross the Somme.

Meanwhile, the French army, too late to save Harfleur, was on the march, now under the command of Charles d'Albret, Constable of France and Jean de Maingre, Marshal of France. It was about 14,000 strong, and it appeared at Blanchetaque to block Henry's crossing. The English did not dare attack a force twice their size across a river, so they made their way inland along the southern bank of the river. On October 19, after 10 days of marching and with their supplies exhausted, they crossed the Somme near its source at Bethencourt and Voyennes. The fords at these villages were in need of repairs, and while the necessary work was being done, the troops were spotted by a band of French cavalry.

At this point, the French seemed reluctant to attack, and for good reason. There was no need to engage the English unless it could not be avoided, and the longer the English were deprived of supplies, the greater their ultimate defeat might be. The priority then was to shadow Henry's army and block its access to Calais while awaiting the arrival of more troops.

There was another reason for not hastily engaging the English. France remembered all too well the devastating effect of English archers at Sluys, Poitiers and Crecy. In all three battles, the longbowmen had decided the outcome, and Henry had 5,000 of them.

The French strategy, sound as it was, was not accepted by a number of commanders, notably Charles, Duke of Orleans, Duke Jean of Bourbon, and John, the Duke of Berry. They considered it scandalous that a huge French army should allow a motley band of half-starved Englishmen to dictate its campaign strategy. At a heated war council, the malcontents gained the upper hand and compelled Constable d'Albret to attack the English. Though his own strategy was wiser and more assured of success, few commanders could have reasonably surmised that a direct assault would disastrously fail. They assumed the English army, driven inland from the Somme, bereft of supplies, low in morale, and having to deal with colder weather, were practically defeated already.

Heralds visited Henry and informed him that the French were prepared to fight him at the time and place of his choosing. The king replied with simulated bravado that he had no wish to do battle, but if the French should block his way to Calais, he would indeed deal them a stinging blow. Inwardly he must have cringed, though now he had one advantage he previously had no reason to believe he might enjoy: the choice of an advantageous position from which to do battle.

As a result, for the time being, the English army was allowed to progress unmolested towards Calais, bypassing Peronne and Arras. On October 24, it reached Blagny, about 30 miles west of Arras, where it sighted the great French host in the valley of the Ternoise. It was completely blocking the road to Calais, and Henry had no choice but to do battle.

That night, the English soldiers confessed their sins to the chaplains in expectation of certain slaughter and sharpened their swords. The cold driving rain was unrelenting and would have done nothing to lift their spirits.

In the French camp there was laughter, drinking, and dancing. The French were always confident of their military superiority, despite several previous demonstrations to the contrary, namely Crecy, Poitiers, and Sluys. And yet, on that eve of the Feast of St Crispin and Crispinian, they did not fear defeat. They possessed one of the largest armies ever to traverse France, and their army had the finest knights (in reputation at least) in all of Christendom. The following day, they assumed they would barely need to strike a blow before the army of the upstart king of England would collapse.

The battle is often interpreted as a monumental failure for French knights and a battlefield strewn with the corpses of the French nobility. The latter is certainly true, but it was not so much a failure of French knighthood since the age of the knight had already passed. A military revolution had begun by the 14th century, with commanders realizing that infantry could be armed to resist cavalry charges. At the Battle of the Golden Spurs in 1302, Flemish burghers had massacred French knights with pole weapons and tactics reminiscent of the ancient Greek phalanxes, and a variety of weapons were designed to unhorse riders and kill cavalry. The bill, a modification of an agricultural implement, was especially favored by the English, and European forces routinely relied on the pike and halberd. The increased importance of infantry meant that cavalry were being gradually relegated to a supportive role, which did not sit well with the higher nobility, who regarded themselves as the traditional warrior class.

Given what happened, it is also important to remember that artillery was not present on the field of Agincourt. Cannons at this time were still rather small and lacked the power to decide battles, though they were beginning to be used in sieges, as at Harfleur. Other forms of artillery, such as catapults, trebuchets, mangonels and ballistae, were not present either. They were most effective in siege warfare and tended to slow armies on the march, and the English were in no state to undertake another punishing siege.

Ironically, the precise location of one of medieval Europe's most famous battles is unknown. The battle is believed to have taken place in a narrow strip of open land between the woods of the villages of Agincourt and Tramecourt, but a lack of archaeological evidence in that area has led some historians to suggest the battle was fought to the west of Agincourt.[85]

What is clear is that King Henry deployed his forces early in the morning of October 25. His troops were positioned across over 2,000 feet of open land, and if they were indeed positioned between the forests of Agincourt and Tramecourt, that position effectively allowed the English to bottleneck the French advance. According to contemporary writers, they were arranged in three groups. Henry, himself, took the center, while the Duke of York took the right and Thomas de Camoys, 1st Baron Camoys, had the left. The longbowmen, commanded by Sir Thomas Erpingham, took positions on both flanks and drove stakes into the ground before them to stave off cavalry charges.

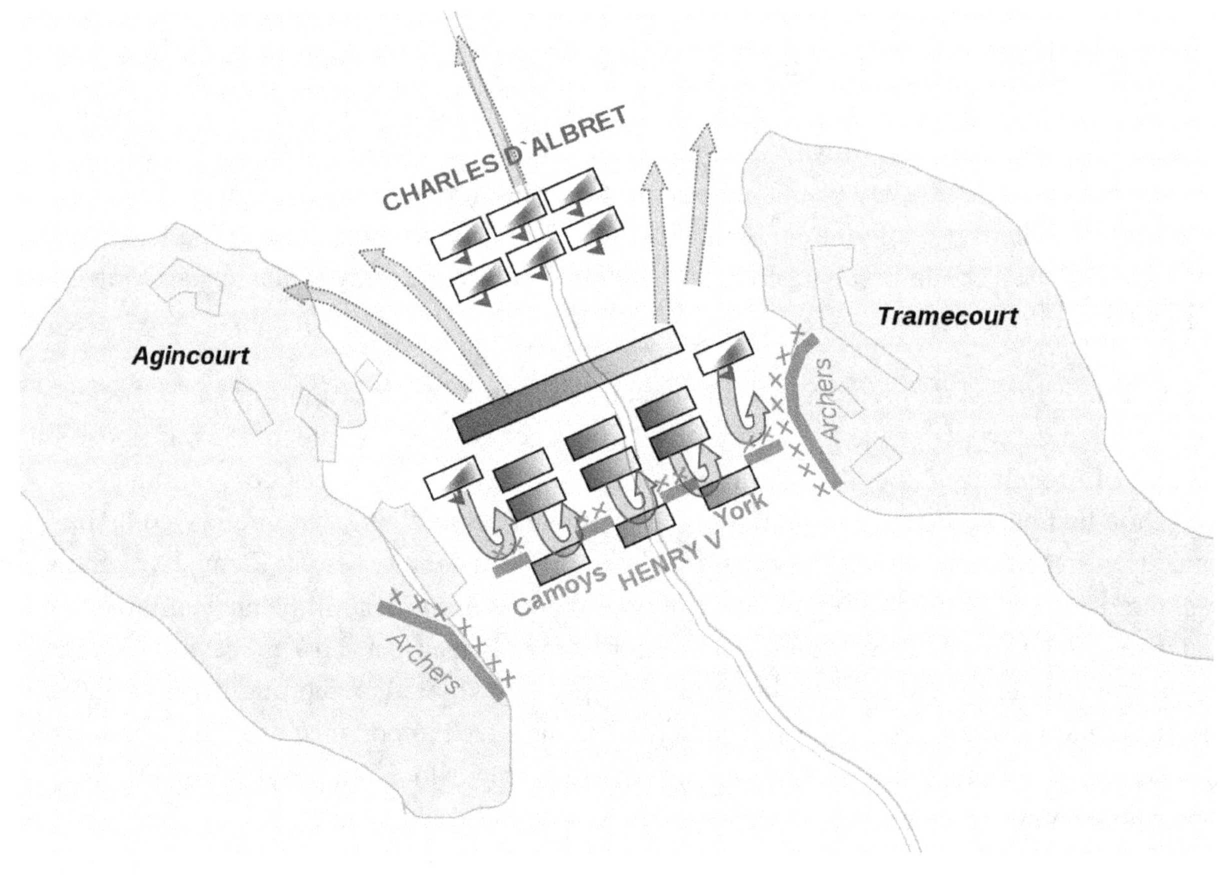

A map of the lines

[85] Sutherland, Tim (17 November 2015). "The Battlefield." In Anne Curry; Malcolm Mercer (eds.). *The Battle of Agincourt*. New Haven & London: Yale University Press.

A modern panorama of the area believed to have been the site of the battle

The French also deployed in three divisions. There was a vanguard followed by the main body, with a rearguard consisting mostly of the mounted retainers of the men-at-arms. In addition, there was a special body of cavalry whose function was to attack the English archers. Their own archers and crossbowmen were deployed, not at the flanks, but at the rear. D'Albret judged them unnecessary, believing – not without justification – that the English would collapse under the French charge. D'Albret and Boucicaut were positioned in the vanguard, along with the bulk of the aristocracy, who demanded positions in the front, which meant almost the entire French command was in or close to the front lines. The rearguard with 10,000 men was largely neglected and had no clear plans for its deployment. Such was the confidence of the French that they had made no provision for an English counterattack.

At sunrise, the French were expecting yet more troops, including 2,000 under Anthony, Duke of Brabant, Duke John V of Brittany with 6,000, and Louis II, Duke of Anjou, with 600. For this reason, the French held off the attack for three hours, content to prevent Henry from escaping. Henry addressed his outnumbered troops, reminding them of past French defeats and asserting the supposed justice of his cause. The famous speech put into Henry's mouth by Shakespeare (*Henry V* Act IV, Scene III) echoes the spirit of the address if not his actual words. Indeed, the king needed to inspire not only his own troops but himself, for it must surely have occurred to him that he might be one of the fallen that day.

At about 9.00 am, the French decided to attack, despite the fact that not all the reinforcements had arrived. As planned, the elite cavalry charged the longbowmen at the English flanks, and it almost immediately became apparent that the move was ill-advised. Though their plate armor protected them from the bulk of the English arrows, the sodden soil from days of heavy rain rapidly turned to mud and slowed their advance. Moreover, when they did reach the longbowmen, they found they could not penetrate the lines of sharpened staves. While in a state of confusion, many lost their horses to arrows and were soon routed. They retreated through the advancing infantry, trampling many underfoot.

At the same time, the French vanguard continued to advance, despite being encumbered by mud. The men-at-arms advanced with their heads bowed for fear that arrows might penetrate the slits in their armor, which was understandable since they were showered in crossfire from the longbowmen, who had not been forced by the cavalry charges to change positions. Though the plated men-at-arms were probably invulnerable to arrow fire, those less protected or wearing poor quality iron were frequently pierced.

As the vanguard approached, the English front line withdrew, so as to entice it into the bottleneck, and just as the French and English men-at-arms were about to engage, the archers abandoned their bows, took up swords, hatchets, and mallets, and fell on the French from the flanks. They were only lightly armored, but the increased mobility was effective against the heavily armored French thanks to the mud, the narrow ground being fought on, and the French's poor vision. The French found themselves being crushed in a bottleneck, unable to lift their weapons and unable to get up out of the mud once they fell. Thousands of men-at-arms surrendered or were killed. Some suffocated in their own armor due to the crushing of the men in the confines of the mud and the battlefield. The dead included D'Albret and John of Alencon.

A 20th century depiction of Henry V fighting at Agincourt

Seeing the carnage, the remnants of the French army hesitated to join in until King Henry V, who fought on the front line, sent its commander a message to retire from the field upon pain of being refused quarter. It did so, followed by the rearguard of retainers. With the French streaming from the battlefield or surrendering, the field, against all odds, belonged to the English. By midday, the battle was won.

For all its savagery and renown, the Battle of Agincourt was not immediately decisive. Though almost all of the French troops were called to arms in the wake of the battle, France was in no danger of conquest. It would be foolish in the extreme to continue a campaign so far beyond the campaigning season, and Paris was strong enough to resist a band of bedraggled Englishmen. In any case, the English were making for Calais, and indeed they continued to that city before they returned to England, where they were hailed as heroes. Harfleur remained safely in English hands.

From one point of view, the Agincourt campaign was a disaster in that it failed to impose a peace on France which forced it to surrender territory, which is what Henry had intended. He had already failed at Harfleur, which held out too long, and had the king returned to England after its fall, he would have lost nothing. Marching north to Calais was definitely a risk, and many might say a rash one. If anything, it was only the pride of the French nobility that allowed him any opportunity to fight. If D'Albret had had his way, the English would have been driven further and further away from Calais until it either surrendered or was crushed in a field far more favorable for the French.

That said, the English did gain something at Agincourt. The defeat of almost the entire French national army struck a terrible blow to the morale of the Armagnacs, the Burgundian faction was careful not to commit too freely to the war against the English, and Duke John of Burgundy was not present at Agincourt. The result essentially made the Burgundians the dominant faction of France.

Somewhat ironically, that would help put into motion the chain of events that led to the end of archers as an integral part of European armies. Arguably the most advanced army before the start of the 16th century was that of Charles the Bold, Duke of Burgundy, who ruled from 1467-1477. He tried to unify his fragmented kingdom by buying up the best soldiers he could, including mounted forces, English longbowmen, Italian condottieri as armored cavalry and infantry, crossbowmen, handgonners, and pikemen. The army was highly organized and blended different types of warriors to take advantage of their best aspects while compensating for each other's weaknesses. His pike formations were mixed with archers and handgonners to provide covering fire and drive away enemies shooting at the formation. Likewise, mounted longbowmen rode with the heavy armored cavalry to provide covering fire from the flanks.

The most advanced wing of Charles the Bold's army was the artillery train. The falcon cannon looked much more like a modern artillery piece than the earlier bombards. Mounted on a wheeled wooden frame with an adjustable barrel, it offered much more maneuverability and accuracy than any competing artillery.

Charles the Bold was ahead of his time, and his ideas would only come to fruition in the 17th century after advances in artillery and musketry made his tactics more practical. Nevertheless, he was a sign of things to come, as warfare had advanced rapidly in 500 years. From the simple feudal forces relying on shield walls and frontal attacks at the Battle of Hastings, armies had developed into professional forces balancing infantry and cavalry with an array of weapons to meet any possible contingency. The next phase of warfare, that of the pike and shot, would be the logical continuation of the developments of the late 15th century.

Meanwhile, despite the longbow's prominence in the Middle Ages, archaeologists have not unearthed any extant longbows dating back before the 15th century.[86] The closest examples of the warbow from its prime are the later versions retrieved from the *Mary Rose*, the warship of Henry VIII which was sunk in 1545 during the Battle of the Solent. 172 bows were retrieved from the supply caches on the ship, with about 80% of them being fully intact.[87] Notably, not all bows in the ship's cache were of the same make - some were D-shaped composite bows (more technically known as plano-convex[88]), while others were more oval shaped.

Modernity

Gunpowder was invented in China in the 8th or 9th century AD, and its use slowly spread through South Asia and the Middle East before making it to Europe in the late 13th century. The famous scholar Francis Bacon gave a recipe for it in a book written in 1267, but for a time it was a mere curiosity. The first record of a cannon in Europe comes from a manuscript written in 1326, which has an illustration showing an armored man with what looks like a slow match lighting a vase-shaped object. An arrow is shooting out of the opening. This crude cannon was called a *pot de fer* in French and *vasi* in Italian. A small specimen weighing 20 pounds has survived in Sweden and is 12 inches long with a 1.5 inch bore. Records show they fired large iron or wooden quarrels with metal fins halfway along the shaft. The rear of the shaft would have been padded to better contain the expanding gases of the exploding powder.

Eventually, medieval engineers developed a new type of cannon in the form of a large cylinder made up of iron bars fused together and strengthened with hoops like a barrel. In fact, this is where the term for the "barrel" of a gun comes from. These devices were called *cannons* or *bombards*. The arrow was replaced with a sphere of stone or lead, both materials being cheap and easy to work. These cannon balls proved to be more aerodynamic and generated more impact than the old-style arrows.

Cannons were quickly brought into use both for sieges and pitched battles. The earliest reference to cannons being used in sieges was the siege of Friuli in Italy in 1331, but it's unclear when they were first used in the field. They may have been used at the battle of Crécy in 1346. It is certain that both the English and French armies were equipped with cannons, but none of the eyewitness accounts of the battle mention them, only a few later histories written decades later.

Bombards grew in size, with some reaching epic proportions. For these giant cannons, the balls would be made of stone because using so much lead would have been prohibitively expensive. This increase in size was encouraged by the development of cheaper gunpowder. Until the late 14th century, saltpeter, a key ingredient in gunpowder, had to be imported from India or found in the rare natural conditions that encouraged its formation. By the end of the 14th century,

---

[86] Loades, *The Longbow*, 7.
[87] France, 'The English Longbow,' 222.
[88] Loades, *The Longbow*, 8.

Europeans had figured out how to make their own saltpeter and production increased to industrial levels.

It wasn't long after the invention of artillery that gunners began to experiment with smaller, handheld black powder weapons. Cannons had the great disadvantage of being slow and cumbersome. There are several reports of artillery not making it to the battle on time, and even the *ribaudiaux* moved more slowly than the average soldier could march. The solution, of course, was to create a small black powder weapon that could be carried by a single man.

European sources first mentioned the widespread use of handgonnes, as they were often called, in the late 14th century, precisely the time when gunpowder became cheaper. These were short metal barrels stuck on the end of wooden hafts that could be tucked under the arm, the powder being lit through a touchhole with the free hand. While they were not terribly accurate, and had a shorter range and slower rate of fire than longbows or crossbows, they had the advantage of being better able to punch through armor than longbows and crossbows. A second advantage was that they were simple to make and use.

Another type of handgonne was the *hackbut*, or hook gun. These generally had long metal stocks fused directly with the barrel. On the bottom of the barrel was a hook that could be braced against a pavise or wall in order to steady the gun and allow more accurate firing. Since they were designed to be braced, *hackbuts* could be larger than regular handgonnes.

Peasants were using handgonnes right from the start. When a group of revolting peasants attacked Huntercombe Manor in England in 1375, they carried with them several handgonnes, and handgonnes soon became a common weapon in peasant rebellions and for urban militias. As cities grew in the 14th century, these militias could be quite large. The one of Strasburg is recorded in 1392 as having 20,000 fully armed men ready for action at a moment's notice. Of course, cities would also be centers of gunpowder and handgonne production.

Handgonnes were limited by their small caliber and modest charge of powder. Early gunpowder was not very powerful, another reason that cannons grew steadily larger in size. Around the beginning of the 15th century, however, chemists developed crumbled and corned powder. By wetting the powder slightly and patting it into a cake to be left to dry, the gunpowder could be stored without the ingredients getting separated or absorbing too much moisture. Not only could it be stored longer than early gunpowder, it could then be crumbled into a large-grain powder with higher surface-to-volume ratio that made it burn quicker. This greatly increased the explosive force.

The increased power made handgonnes much deadlier, and by the late 15th century they had evolved into something more resembling the familiar shape of a musket, with a long barrel set into a wooden stock that could be brought to the shoulder. This made the weapon easier to aim and more accurate. Most were still lit by hand with a slow match, but early in the century there were already experiments with making crude levers that could bring the match down by pressing with a single finger as both hands gripped the handgonne. A proper matchlock mechanism fired by a button appeared in the late 15th century, and the more familiar trigger was introduced in the early 16th century.

It would not be until the full adoption of the matchlock and further improvements in gunpowder that full plate armor would disappear. Armor was still useful against other weapons, and until the full development of the matchlock, handgonnes remained inaccurate, short-range devices. They tended to be used in conjunction with other weapons, with handgonners most commonly being teamed up with crossbowmen. Bows were more accurate and had a faster rate of fire, and though arrows were less likely to punch through armor, they could provide a good covering fire, harassing and slowly diminishing the enemy until they got close enough for the handgonners to deliver a deadly volley.

Handgonnes, even in their simple form, spread quickly throughout Europe. Many castle owners modified the arrow slits on their walls, cutting circular holes in them to accommodate handgonnes or small cannons. By the late 15th century, handgonners had become a major part of the leading armies. An account about the army from Milan in 1482 mentions 1,250 handgonners, 233 crossbowmen, and 352 arquebusiers. The arquebus was an early matchlock with a spring-loaded lock activated with a button. When the button was pressed, the lock would bring the slow match down on the firing pan and light the powder. These were expensive to make, so for a time the more primitive handgonnes remained in use for the bulk of the men. Bows were on their way out.

In England, bows were pretty much out of style by the English Civil War, but they were occasionally used to target messengers traveling between forces, such as during the Siege of Gloucester in 1643.[89] Before then, though, the bow still had its share of defenders. Most vocal among them was the traditionalist military historian, Sir John Smythe, who lauded the "English bowes" over those produced in Africa and Asia, because they "exceed and excell al other bowes used by all forren nations not only in substance & strength, but also in the length & bignes of the arrows."[90]

Nonetheless, by the end of the 15th century, Smyth became embroiled in debates with military veterans who wished to see the weapon done away with in favor of newer technology. These included Humphrey Barwick, who fought in the Siege of Leith, as well as the military theorist Roger Williams, who fought in several battles in the Dutch Revolt and the French Wars of Religion. These soldiers wished to see the bow severely restricted or altogether banned.

This period saw the turning of public and political opinion regarding longbows. Even Smythe

---

[89] Peter Gaunt, The English Civil War: A Military History, (London/New York: I. B. Tauris, 2014), 115.
[90] Rogers, 'Development,' 323.

did not advocate for the entire English army to be armed with only bows. By this point in time, the firearm had been widely adopted, and it has been suggested by Gervase Phillips that the longbow's unique cultural influence and its centrality to tactical practice ensured that it was difficult to completely get rid of, even in the face of superior technology.[91]

It is also important to note that the debate over firearms and bows did not come out of a vacuum. For decades prior to the turn of the 16th century, many officials had insisted that the halberd should be replaced by the pike as the officiant phalanx weapon.[92] Technological developments in every sphere demanded a radical change to occur soon within the English military scheme, but now was not the time for it. Furthermore, for much of the 16th century, the English enjoyed a period of relative peace.

Once the wars against the Spanish broke out, especially under the rule of Queen Elizabeth I, the need for technological development came about once again. Indeed, the initial engagements between the English and Spanish were abysmally lopsided. The Spanish had superior training and arms, whilst the English barely had a standing army. Following early defeats, the troops of Robert Dudley, Earl of Leicester, received ample training with new types of firearms. Through Leicester, the "New Discipline," as he called it, needed to be implemented due to the obvious success that it enjoyed on the continent. The military historian Roger Williams was quickly converted to the "New Discipline" and explained his position in his work *A Brief Discourse on War* (1590): "In our ancient wars, our enemies used crossbows, and such shoots; few, or any at all had the use of long bows as we had. Wherefore none could compare with us for shot: but God forbid we should try our bows with their muskets and calivers, without the like shot to answer them. I do not doubt but all, honourable and others, notwithstanding some will contrary it, although they never saw the true trial of those weapons belonging either to horse or foot; alleging antiquity without other reasons, saying, we carried arms before they were born.... True it is, long experience requires age, age without experience requires small discipline. Therefore we are deceived, to judge men expert because they carried arms 40 years, and never in action 3 years, during their lives counting all together."[93]

Williams was convinced that archery would be ineffective against armored cavalry, especially if the latter was backed up by musketeers. His argument, therefore, stemmed from the desire to see England catch up to its rivals in Europe in terms of technology. Smythe, in his counterarguments, noted that the critics of the bow were not veterans of high discipline, pitched battles, and that the relative peace in the early Tudor period had led to a "decay of military exercise and science."[94] Smythe pointed out the drawbacks of arquebuses that longbows did not

---

[91] Gervase Phillips, 'Longbow and Hackbutt: Weapons Technology and Technology Transfer in Early Modern England,' Technology and Culture, Volume 40, Number 3 (July 1999): 577.

[92] Thomas Esper, 'The Replacement of the Longbow by Firearms in the English Army,' Technology and Culture, Volume 6, Number 3 (Summer, 1965): 384.

[93] Ibid, 385.

[94] Ibid, 388.

have - they often overheated prematurely, had less range, and were only effective at half that range.[95] Along with that, bows were far cheaper to produce, and the well-entrenched history of English archery ensured there was no shortage of bowyers to do the work. Another advantage the bow had over its technologically superior rival was its rate of fire, as longbowmen could fire up to six arrows a minute while the primitive firearms could only fire one bullet in the same time,[96] an observation also made by Benjamin Franklin in the 18th century.[97]

Smythe also capitalized on the fear that archers instilled in the enemy. English captains adored the use of special "flight arrows" - arrows far too small to do any serious damage, but used frequently to cause chaos among enemy ranks. The high volume of flight arrows would make the enemy forces think they were at great risk and that the archers were firing more arrows than what was believed to be possible. This would cause an attacking force to break rank and, hopefully, retreat, or to attempt a desperate advance that would put the infantry in more danger. This occurred at the Battle of the Spurs in 1513 where English archers used showers of light arrows to cause panic among the advancing French, compelling them to abandon their advance and flee in a disorderly fashion.[98]

As noted earlier, there were several battles where archers complemented men using other weapons, including the guns. The Venetians were able to draw upon a large body of skilled archers and used them to protect arquebusiers as they reloaded, and this became so effective that Venetian galleys continued to have complements of archers well into the 17th century. The 16th century Italian mercenary Giovacchino de Comiano recalled how his favorite tactic was to outflank English troops using both arquebusiers and archers to allow for a continual rate of fire.[99] The English were no different in their insistence to continue using the bow and arrow, despite its inevitable decline, because put simply, the combination of harassing fire and long range and stopping fire at short range was quite effective.

As this makes clear, there is no reason to think that as the English began to adopt muskets and arquebuses into their militaries, the longbow simply vanished. Instead, the two were always intended to be utilized with each other, which helps explain why Henry VIII insisted on using archers on his prized flagship the *Mary Rose*. He did go out of his way to employ expensive foreign arquebusiers, but encouraged his subjects not to do the same. Henry was a patron for archery and only adopted the early firearms with reluctance as new conflicts brewed on the horizon.

Despite this early intention, it is clear that the great successes of early firearms led to a further decline in longbows being used in the English military, to the point where the warbow began to

---

[95] Ibid, 389.
[96] Phillips, 'Longbow and Hackbutt,' 581.
[97] Esper, 'Replacement,' 382.
[98] Phillips, 'Longbow and Hackbutt,' 582.
[99] Phillips, 'Longbow and Hackbutt,' 582-83.

become a liability. For example, in 1534, Henry VIII was informed from the continent that "arquebuses are now made here which give double the stroke of the hand gun."[100] Inevitably, the loudness of early handguns also made men weary of attacking snipers and other men armed with guns. A natural sense of awe and dread filled the minds of those who, for all they knew, saw their enemies as holding small cannons in their hands. In 1544, during the Siege of Montreuil, a Welsh captain with over 20 years of experience was stationed with the garrison at Calais, and he despairingly noted, "I never saw Welshmen or Englishmen so bad hearted or so unventuresome as I saw at this time. Not a single one of them would dare to go near where the handguns were shooting at us."[101]

There was also an evolving class situation that affected the bow's popularity. The 1540s saw a decline in the availability of able-bodied men for the English army, mostly due to the "sweating sickness epidemic." Furthermore, the aforementioned class struggle against a ruling gentry was beginning to break down in the Tudor period. Although class struggle continued and was, in some ways, exacerbated during the Tudor period, many yeomen began to view military service in a different light than how their ancestors did. Tenants no longer felt an obligation to follow their wealthy landlords into war. They had now gained the confidence to challenge these archaic notions and establish their socio-economic independence. It follows that these yeomen felt no obligation to practice with their bows, as they would find no practical use for them.[102] With that, the supply of archers diminished, and it was only a matter of time before more practical firearms, which had already been in development for the past century, would become dominant in English militaries.

The diminishing ruling gentry also appeared to have taken advantage of the emergence of the musket and arquebus as superior weapons. Not only would it deprive the lower classes of their long-held means by which they would usurp class authority, but it would also give the ruling gentry a reason not to hire the yeoman archers as cheap soldiers. Those who believed in the inherent superiority of the firearm over the bow argued that the new arquebuses "were considered too dangerous for the great multitude of the easily disaffected."[103] This was not entirely untrue, as a 1540 Westminster statue was issued limiting the use of arquebuses in poorer parts of cities and towns as people were discharging their weapons and people were getting killed.[104]

As Phillips concluded regarding the class situation: "The fate of the bow became linked to the fate of the poor, whether threatened by enclosure or some other manifestation of privileged greed. Thus the blue-blooded Smyth's pro-archery polemic of 1590 was marked by a paternalistic concern for England's yeoman and a ferocious assault on captains who sent their

---

[100] Ibid, 580.
[101] Ibid, 580-81.
[102] Ibid, 586.
[103] Ibid, 583.
[104] Ibid.

men to certain death in order to pocket their wages as deadpay"[105]

In the 20th century, a renewed interest in toxophily (archery crafting and practice) surged. Prior to the 1920s, scientific and scholarly literature on the subject of archery was scarce, but various analyses were undertaken to estimate the effectiveness of longbows, with many mathematicians and physicists trying to determine the facts. The Torsion spring bow model provided by Denny (but pioneered by earlier scientists of history) estimates that the kinetic energy generated by a longbow with the appropriate dimensions could, theoretically, use 100% of all the energy produced in the string tension. This includes the additional energy left over in the archer's draw arm, which is also transferred from the strings to the arrow upon release. Given appropriate conditions for usage, *all* bows may be considered to be roughly 98% (is not 100%) effective mathematically.[106]

To this day, tens of thousands of archery clubs exist, most prominently, of course, in the United Kingdom.

Online Resources

Other books about medieval history by Charles River Editors

Further Reading

Anonymous. (2007) 'The Welsh and English Longbow,' Hampton Roads Military History, Volume 1.

Anonymous. (2005). Review of *From Hastings to the Mary Rose: the Great Warbow*. Matthew Strickland and Robert Hardy, Contemporary Review, Volume 287.

Ayton, A., Preston, P. (2007). *The Battle of Crécy, 1346*. Woodbridge, Suffolk: Boydell Press.

Bruce, A. (1981). *A Bibliography of British Military History: From the Roman Invasions to the Restoration, 1660*. London/Paris/New York: Saur.

Capwell, T. (2013). Review of *From Hastings to the Mary Rose: The Great Warbow*, Matthew Strickland and Robert Hardy, Journal of Conflict Archaeology, Volume 2, Number 1.

Denny, M. (2007). Ingenium: Five Machines That Changed the World, (Baltimore: John Hopkins University Press.

Esper, T. (1965). 'The Replacement of the Longbow by Firearms in the English Army,' Technology and Culture, Volume 6, Number 3.

---

[105] Ibid, 585.
[106] Denny, *Ingenium*, 11-14.

France, J. (2017). 'The English Longbow, War, and Administration,' Journal of Medieval Military History, Vol. 15.

Gaunt, P. (2014). *The English Civil War: A Military History*. London/New York: I. B. Tauris.

Halfond G. I. (2015). *The Medieval Way of War: Studies in Medieval Military History in Honor of Bernard S. Bachrach*. London: Routledge.

Hardy, R. (1995). *Longbow: A Social and Military History*. London: Sutton Publishing.

Loades, M. (2019). *War Bows: Longbow, Crossbow, Composite Bow, and Japanese Yumi*. Oxford: Bloomsbury.

Loades, M (2013). *The Longbow*. Oxford: Osprey.

Phillips, G. (1999). 'Longbow and Hackbutt: Weapons Technology and Technology Transfer in Early Modern England,' Technology and Culture, Volume 40, Number 3.

Rogers, C (1998). 'The Efficacy of the English Longbow: A Reply to Kelly DeVries,' War in History, Volume 5, No. 2.

Rogers, C. (2011). The Development of the Longbow in Late Medieval England and 'Technological Determinism,' Journal of Medieval History, Volume 37, Issue 3.

Villalon, A., Kagay, D. (2008). *The Hundred Years War (Part II)*, History of Warfare Volume 51. Leiden/Boston: Brill.

Wailly, H. (1987). Crécy 1346: Anatomy of a Battle. Poole: Blandford Press.

Wierer U, Arrighi S, Bertola S, Kaufmann G, Baumgarten B, Pedrotti A, et al. (2018). 'The Iceman's Lithic Toolkit: Raw Material, Technology, Typology and Use.' PLOS ONE 13(6).